The Legend of
Saint Edmund

ISBN: 978-1-9997509-0-9

The cover picture and all the other pictures in this book are from British Library Harley Manuscript 2278: John Lydgate's Lives of St Edmund and St Fremund, in the presentation copy for Henry VI, England (probably Bury St Edmunds) between 1434 and 1439.

www.bl.uk

The Legend of St Edmund

by

John Lydgate

In a Modern English Version

by

Simon Webb

Also from the Langley Press

The Legend of St Alban
In Search of St Alban
A Little Book of English Saints
The Legend of St Cuthbert
In Search of the Northern Saints
In Search of the Celtic Saints
In Search of Bede
An African Testament: The Heart of the Kebra Nagast
Nicholas Breakspear: The Pope from England
Aaron of Lincoln

For free downloads and more from the Langley Press, please
visit our website at http://tinyurl.com/lpdirect

Contents

Henry VI praying at the shrine of St Edmund

Introduction

In Anglo-Saxon times, there were bears and wolves and worse in the English countryside, so one can imagine the feelings of a blind man and his son who found themselves lost in a Suffolk forest some time during the early years of the tenth century.

They needed to find shelter fast – but there seemed to be nothing for miles around but trees. At last they came upon a mysterious little wooden building, and, no doubt relieved, they let themselves in. In the utter blackness, either the blind man or his son stumbled on a low platform that stood inside. The son was unnerved, but his father, with the insight blind people often seem to have in old stories, reassured him that their host was a good man, and would neither hurt them, nor resent their staying the night.

Using the edge of the platform as their pillow, the pair drifted into sleep, the younger man no doubt wondering as he dozed off who this 'host' was that his father had mentioned. Surely the two of them were the only people in the place?

In the night, the young man was unnerved again, this time by a bright light that woke him up and filled the little house, but seemed to come from nowhere. Again, his father reassured him that their host would let no harm come to them.

7

In the morning, both father and son woke up to find that they had been sleeping in a little woodland chapel that had been built around the tomb of St Edmund, king and martyr of East Anglia, who had been slaughtered by Vikings in the previous century. Both men could see this, because the father's sight had been miraculously restored overnight. He had been right to say that their host would look after them.

The story reminds us of a lot of things about the Anglo-Saxon world in which it is supposed to have happened, and the later medieval world that cherished and perpetuated such stories. In those days, there were still forests big enough to get lost in in England, and nature had a rather more threatening aspect than it has for English people today.

The story also reminds us that, although their souls were supposed to be in heaven, the dead bodies of saints and martyrs were thought to possess miraculous powers, and to be surrounded by an aura of holiness that some people were able to detect. And both the bodies and souls of long-dead Christian saints were thought to be able to play an active part in the lives of the living; generating strange lights, changing the weather, and both curing the deserving sick and causing sudden illnesses, including bouts of severe madness, in people who were less deserving.

As we will see in the following pages, long-dead saints also had a legal role as protectors and patrons of parts of Britain, which were supposed to have special status because of their presence. St Edmund's status as both a saint and a king is also a reminder of the special relationship between the Christian religion and the English monarchy, both before and after the time when only one monarch ruled over the whole of England.

In his play *Hamlet*, William Shakespeare has the usurper Claudius remind us that 'divinity doth hedge a king', and the holy powers supposed to be possessed by English monarchs were, until the early eighteenth century, reflected in the ceremony of touching for the King's Evil, a form of scrofula which, it was believed, could be cured by the royal touch alone.

Among British royal saints are Edward the Confessor (who is mentioned in the following narrative), King Oswald of Northumbria, and Queen Margaret of Scotland. One English monarch who was never officially made into a saint, despite posthumous miracles, a popular following and much lobbying of the Pope, was the fifteenth-century King Henry VI, known as Henry of Windsor, who is also known to have touched for the King's Evil.

King Henry VII, our first Tudor monarch, tried very hard to have Henry VI canonised, because the earlier Henry was the son of Henry V, and Henry VII's claim to the throne was partly based on the fact that his own father, Edmund Tudor, was the son of Henry V's widow by Owen Tudor. To be related to a king was good, but to be related to a royal saint was even better.

Although Shakespeare, in his three plays covering the chaotic reign of Henry VI, certainly presents the king as a man too pious to rule a country, Bertram Wolffe, in his 1981 biography of the sixth Henry, shows that he was probably not exceptionally pious or monkish, but merely weak, ineffectual, lacking in intelligence, and prone to prolonged periods of mental illness.

One piece of evidence that was supposed to prove that Henry VI was saintly was the fact that, as a boy of twelve, he had spent several months at the abbey of St Edmundsbury. Wolffe asserts that the young king and his court had been dumped there by the ruling council to sponge off the enforced hospitality of the abbot, because money was very tight at the time. During this sojourn, which stretched from Christmas 1433 to Easter 1434, Abbot William commissioned one of his monks, a poet called John Lydgate, to write the lives of St Edmund and his contemporary St

Fremund, in English verse. The following is a re-telling of the story of Edmund as presented by Lydgate, whose own version was, as he himself tells us, supposed to represent the 'substance' of an early Latin account.

As a poet, John Lydgate, who may have been in his early sixties when Henry VI was at St Edmundsbury, has always suffered by comparison with his older contemporary Geoffrey Chaucer, author of the celebrated *Canterbury Tales*. Like Chaucer, Lydgate wrote in Middle English, the English of the Middle Ages, that is recognisable as English but has so many unfamiliar words and spellings that readers generally have to be taught how to make sense of it, and need experience to feel at home with it and read it fluently.

Lydgate admired Chaucer and was heavily influenced by his poetry, but seldom managed to recapture the vitality of the older poet's best work. Lydgate also committed the terrible sin of writing far too many long poems. His account of Edmund and Fremund stretches to over thirty-six thousand lines, as does his *Fall of Princes*. His prodigious *Siege of Thebes* is over forty-seven thousand lines long. The size of his output means that it is difficult for modern critics to arrive at a really informed assessment of Lydgate as a poet. This and the uneven quality of his verse persuaded the ill-tempered eighteenth-century antiquary Joseph Ritson to call Lydgate 'a voluminous, prosaick and drivelling monk'. Suffice it to say, Lydgate was very much respected as a poet by his contemporaries − hence distinguished and lucrative commissions such as the one that found him writing his verse lives of Edmund and Fremund for King Henry VI.

Some of the qualities that may make Lydgate seem tiresome to some modern readers may be exactly the ones that made his work strike a chord back in the fifteenth century. He will often break off from his narrative to devote several verses to, for instance, the miraculous things that 'grace' can do. When one of his characters makes a pious speech, or utters a spontaneous prayer, this can also go on rather too long. Lydgate's descriptions of such things as the excellent qualities of a saint can also be tedious and repetitive.

In an account of Lydgate's career as a writer given in the introduction to a selection from his poems published in 1966, Lydgate's verse hagiographies, or lives of the saints, are characterised as likely to be of little interest to modern readers, who are more used to reading more factual histories or biographies in the modern style. I hope that John Norton-Smith, the editor of the 1966 selection and the author of its introduction, was wrong in implying that the often surreal and whimsical tales that surround some Christian saints are of little interest to modern readers.

It is certainly true that much of what Lydgate writes about St Edmund cannot be accepted as historical fact. In fact the reliable historical information we have about this ninth-century Anglo-Saxon king of East Anglia could probably be fitted onto one side of A4 paper, double-spaced, with room to spare. As the Victorian philosopher Thomas Carlyle tells us in his 1843 book *Past and Present*, it is likely that Edmund, whom Carlyle insists on repeatedly calling a 'landlord', was probably just a virtuous local magnate of some kind who was fondly remembered and gradually turned into a saint by later generations:

there dwelt a man in these parts, of the name of Edmund, King, Landlord, Duke or whatever his title was, of the Eastern Counties; —and a very singular man and landlord he must have been. For his tenants, it would appear, did not complain of him in the least; his labourers did not think of burning his wheatstacks, breaking into his game-preserves; very far the reverse of all that. Clear evidence [. . .] exists that, on the contrary, they honoured, loved, admired this ancient Landlord to a quite astonishing degree,—and indeed at last to an immeasurable and inexpressible degree; for, finding no limits or utterable words for their sense of his worth, they took to beatifying and adoring him! 'Infinite admiration,' we are taught, 'means worship.' [. . .] His Life has become a poetic, nay a religious *Mythus* [. . .]

In much the same way that Carlyle introduces such Victorian concerns as the activities of rick-burners and poachers into the passage above, John Lydgate, in his account of this 'singular man and landlord' gives him, his court and even what we would now call his Viking enemies some decidedly fifteenth-century accoutrements. Edmund wears coat-armour emblazoned with a type of heraldry that would have been very modern to Lydgate, and Ivar, Edmund's Viking nemesis, campaigns like Henry V, putting up pavilions at the end of a day's march.

Lydgate's anachronisms are in the same general class as Shakespeare's ancient Romans throwing up their hats in celebration (in *Coriolanus*) and his Cleopatra having a corset with ribbons. They do, however, add to the air of unreality that pervades his poem, as do his inclusion of some very unlikely stories that do not even count as miracle-stories. One of these is surely the tale of Lothbrok, who is happier as one of Edmund's courtiers than he was as king of Denmark.

In fact many aspects of Lothbrok's story, as presented by Lydgate, seem unlikely. Why, on a hawking expedition, would Lothbrok suddenly rush out ahead of his companions, and then lie down and go to sleep in a boat? When Lothbrok, who becomes a favourite courtier of Edmund, is murdered, we are supposed to believe that Edmund does not have Bern, the murderer, executed or imprisoned, but casts him adrift on the North Sea in the same boat. We are then supposed to believe that this boat somehow found its way back to Lothbrok's kingdom, where his two odious sons, Ivar and Ubba, are waiting.

Another unlikely aspect of the story is that Edmund is

not a home-grown English king, but a native of Saxony who is chosen for the job on his merits. This idea may be derived from a misreading of a source that states that Edmund was from an old Saxon family.

If we take the story of Edmund's German origins seriously, then some time spent reading between the lines of Lydgate's story quickly reveals parts of a possible alternative, half-concealed version of events. The author is clear that Edmund arrived in England with a large army, and we are also told that he established the town of Hunstanton where he landed. He was also forced to wait for a year until he could be accepted as king and crowned, during which time he memorised the psalter. Could it be that this story contains the shadowy form of the true history of a German invasion of East Anglia in Anglo-Saxon times? Was Hunstanton a fortress the invader established as a base of operations while he gained allies among the English, besieged key settlements, and generally softened up the opposition?

Another feature of Lydgate's treatment of the Edmund story that makes it more like a modern fantasy novel than a work of history is the poet's failure to include certain known historical facts, for instance about the Viking invasion of England by Ivar and Ubba, and the movements of Edmund's mortal remains.

The way that successive writers like Lydgate and the authors of his sources added to the slender story of King Edmund makes the saint's legend read rather like that of an earlier British hero, King Arthur. Again, very little is known about this man, but there are endless myths, poems, novels, films and even TV series.

An aspect of Edmund's *mythos* that Lydgate seems to be particularly keen on is his supposed virginity – his status as a 'maiden'. This idea is probably based on the fact that among the few hard scraps of information we have about this king, there is no mention of his having married or fathered children.

Lydgate and the other monkish authors who treated of Edmund, who were all supposed to be celibate themselves, seem to have seized on this gap in our information make Edmund even purer and more holy, although in terms of *realpolitik* a celibate king could create profound problems, since a key duty of a medieval monarch was to present his kingdom with at least one heir.

Some of the problems that surrounded the reign of the doomed King Richard II, a patron of Chaucer, were made worse by his failure to get his first wife pregnant, and his second marriage to a mere child who was far too young to have any children. The celebrated Wilton Diptych, a masterpiece of medieval art that is now in the English National Gallery in London, depicts Richard, who may have remained celibate during his first marriage for religious reasons, with John the Baptist, Edward the Confessor and St Edmund. Some think that Richard may have remained celibate during his marriage because of his religious devotion to Edward the Confessor, who is thought to have done the same thing.

Besides procreation, another duty of medieval monarchs that was not entirely consistent with sainthood was warfare. Royal saints like St Oswald of Northumbria embraced war against British pagans as a kind of holy duty, but Sigeberht, another king of East Anglia who ruled over two hundred years before Edmund, renounced violence altogether. Sigeberht abdicated and became a monk, possibly in a monastery he himself had had built at Bury St Edmunds. When he was forced to return to the battlefield, he refused to arm himself, and went into battle carrying only a staff. His martyrdom is thought to have happened circa 634 CE.

Lydgate's version of Edmund's life has the saint renouncing violence after he becomes horrified by the results of a prolonged battle he himself has won: but there is no question of his becoming a monk, like Sigeberht. An interesting factor in Edmund's remorse is that, instead of feeling pleased that he has slaughtered pagans, he feels especially sorry for them because he believes that they are bound to spend eternity in hell.

Remorse after violence appears again in Lydgate's St Edmund when Bishop Leofric is struck with guilt after ordering the executions of eight thieves who tried to raid Edmund's shrine. This Leofric should not be confused with Leofric the Sheriff, who is attacked by a demon after violating the sanctuary offered to fugitives at the shrine of St Edmund.

Lydgate's apparent promotion in his poem of what we would now call pacifism may have been informed by his sense of the horrors of the war the English had then long been fighting against the French. Among the inevitable atrocities of this war were the execution of the saintly, martial virgin Joan of Arc just two years before Lydgate sat down to write his poem. Because of the war Henry VI's father Henry V had fought against the French, it was possible for his son, the recipient of Lydgate's poem, to be crowned king of both England and France – but at what cost in human life?

Lydgate is keen to present Edmund as an accomplished military leader, capable of victory in battle against a formidable opponent, but the poet is also aware that Jesus Christ is the Prince of Peace, and that a truly saintly man will not get involved in war. One way to square that circle is to present the interesting spectacle of a victorious warrior-king who renounces violence.

Lydgate is extremely unlikely to have known this, but Edmund's sudden conversion to pacifism is mirrored in the case of Ashoka, an emperor of India who lived in the third century BCE. After a victorious war against a people called

15

the Kalingas, Ashoka became horrified by the carnage he had caused, embraced a very peaceable form of Buddhism, and ushered in an age of peace, prosperity and religious tolerance.

If the poet John Lydgate had hoped that young Henry VI's double coronation would precede a time of prolonged peace, then his hopes were to be frustrated. Not only did the war in France continue: twenty-three years after the twelve year-old Henry VI had stayed as Bury St Edmunds, the Wars of the Roses began – wars that were partly caused by the weakness of Henry, if not his supposed excessive piety, and which were to stretch over more than thirty years.

The legends that were attached to the core story of King Edmund during the Middle Ages may have been derived from earlier saintly tales. The story of Edmund's coffin refusing to be moved to St Paul's in London, and suddenly becoming as heavy and immovable as a mountain, is similar to a story about another Anglo-Saxon saint, St Cuthbert. The cart on which Cuthbert's coffin was being transported became immovable because, it seems, he wanted to go to Durham, where he now lies in the famous Norman cathedral. Only when the monks who were escorting the saint tried to take him in that direction did the cart become light and moveable again.

Aspects of two stories that John Lydgate applies to Edmund's departure from his alleged home in Saxony, and his first arrival in England, may ultimately be derived from very ancient, pre-Christian tales about gods and demi-gods. When Edmund leaves Saxony, there is excessive weeping; and when he arrives in England for the first time, springs of water miraculously appear, and the fields for miles around grow more fertile. These accounts make Edmund resemble ancient Gods like Adonis, from the classical tradition of ancient Greece and Rome, who was supposed to descend into the underworld, accompanied by much weeping, for part of the year, then emerge to revive nature and the fertility of the crops. The fact that Edmund is both born, and crowned king of East Anglia, at Christmas, may also have a deep, mythic significance, linking him to pagan mid-winter festivals, as well as the birth of Jesus.

This combination of a young king, fertile crops and a thriving kingdom makes Edmund the opposite of the Fisher King, a figure who features in the Grail legends. The Fisher King is the guardian of the Holy Grail, which is kept in his castle, Corbenic; but he suffers from a terrible wound that means that he cannot walk or even stand up properly, and the only activity he can engage in is to sit in a boat and fish. A significant part of some versions of this legend is that, because of his own sickness, the Fisher King's lands, the health of which is mystically linked to his own medical condition, are barren and fruitless.

In the Edmund legend, the equivalent of the Fisher King may be King Offa of East Anglia, an elderly king who has lost hope of ever producing an heir, who arranges for Edmund, his nephew, to travel from his home in Saxony to inherit his kingdom. This King Offa should not be confused with King Offa of Mercia, who is thought to have built Offa's Dyke.

A characteristic of the barren, god-forsaken lands that are sometimes found to be ruled by ailing or evil monarchs in Arthurian legends are the dangerous wildernesses that dominate them. When the ailing king is healed, or there is a beneficial regime change, the wilderness is tamed and becomes safe and fruitful. Similar ideas are reflected in the tale of the wolf that is said to have guarded Edmund's severed head in the forest until it was recovered by loyal searchers. This wild animal, a member of a species which was really dreaded by medieval people (Lydgate reminds us that wolves sometimes became man-eaters) becomes tame thanks to Edmund's influence, and serves a useful purpose as a guard-dog.

In other knightly legends, lands are barren because a dragon has laid waste to them. This situation can only be remedied by the intervention of a knight; and throughout his version of the life of St Edmund, John Lydgate insists that his protagonist is the perfect royal knight, as well as being a king and a saint. The dragons in Edmund's story are the Vikings, but, perhaps because of the Christian character of the story, Edmund does not slay the dragon and then ride off into the sunset with some damsel riding side-saddle behind him. He dies, but his sacrifice is understood to bring lasting benefits to his lands.

Although Lydgate, perhaps unwittingly, stumbles onto some deep mythic material in his re-telling of the Edmund legends, he is also concerned with some more mundane matters. The last of his three books, which deals with St Edmund's miracles, makes it very clear that, saintly as he was, Edmund was not above using miraculous powers to punish people who offended him, especially if their offence included some infringement of the privileged status of East Anglia as a region under his special protection as a saint.

King Sweyn of Denmark's attempts to mistreat the East Anglians and break their region's exemption from tax, as well as his inhospitable treatment of one of Edmund's friends in the land of the living, convinces the saint to doff his snow-white saintly robes, dress up as a knight again and take direct action. Likewise, attempts by both knights and common thieves to steal from the saint are punished by punitive miracles. As we have seen, when the bishop of London attempts to steal the saint himself, the coffin becomes too heavy to move.

It is possible that Lydgate's use of examples of how offenders against Edmund and his people came to grief were aimed at the child-king, Henry VI, for whom he is supposed to have written his poem. Did he hope that a superstitious fear of miracles would persuade the cash-strapped monarch to keep his hands off the revenues and privileges of the church?

Bishop Alphun of London's scheme to abduct Edmund's corpse is understandable, given the immense prestige the body of a popular saint count confer on a church or cathedral in medieval times. The presence of such holy bones could lead to the church becoming a centre of pilgrimage – pilgrimages being the medieval equivalents, in many ways, of modern tourist holidays. In the same way that crowds of tourists can add to the income and profitability of certain places, so pilgrims brought serious money into many towns and cities in Europe. In England these places included Canterbury, where the cathedral houses the remains of the martyr Thomas Becket; and Durham, home to Cuthbert and Bede. In the case of Durham, the venerable Anglo-Saxon St Bede is only in the cathedral because his bones were, in effect, stolen away from their original resting-place, much as Bishop Alphun of London planned to steal Edmund's bones.

If the presence of a saint's bones could boost the prestige of a church or cathedral, the presence of royal bones could do the same. A place that proudly boasts a coat of arms featuring three crowns, like Edmund's coat of arms, is Tynemouth, where three kings are said to have been buried.

The bones of a royal saint could indeed boost the prestige of a church, cathedral, town, city or region, and the idea of kings and queens who could become saints boosted the prestige of the idea of Christian kingship. As we have seen, the first Tudor king, Henry VII, petitioned the Pope to have Henry VI made into a saint, no doubt because the presence of a holy king on his family tree would make his own claim to the English throne look more legitimate.

Perhaps for similar reasons, King Alfred the Great of Wessex began to mint coins commemorating the life of Edmund, something which Houghton, in his 1970 book on the saint, identifies as the moment when the martyr was officially recognised as a saint. In time, Edmund stopped being just a local saint and became the first patron saint of the whole of England. He was, however, replaced by St George, whose flag, a slender red cross on a white background, still appears all over the country when the national soccer team is facing an important game.

As recently as 2013 there was a campaign to reinstate Edmund as patron saint of England but, like a similar attempt in 2006, this was not successful.

In my abridged prose re-telling of John Lydgate's account of St Edmund, I have pruned back the poet's long-winded digressions in order to let the central narrative show through. I hope this will allow modern readers to see how the poet handles much of the narrative content with skill, discernment and some humour. To give an idea of Lydgate's original, I have included a verse in Middle English, with a modern spelling version, and a Latin prayer with a modern English translation, as appendices. The verse, concerning Ivar's retreat from a battle against Edmund, struck me as one of the best in the poem.

Where Lydgate is a little obscure, I have sometimes inserted a few words by way of explanation. In re-telling Lydgate's story of a Fleming who tried to steal part of Edmund's shrine by biting it off, for example, I have given the extra detail that parts of the medieval shrine were made out of gold, a metal so soft that the unsuccessful thief may really have believed that he could steal a piece using only his teeth.

I have changed some names in the text to the version most frequently used by modern historians, so that, for instance, Lydgate's 'Hynguar' becomes 'Ivar'.

Although they sometimes coincide with places where

Lydgate starts a new chapter, the divisions into chapters are mine, as are the chapter headings.

SW, Durham, 2018

The Legend of
Saint Edmund

Lydgate's Prologue

I will begin by describing the standards of St Edmund, virgin, king and martyr. Both of his standards reflect his great virtues – the virtues that enabled him to banish the serpent's venom from his kingdom. Both were designed with great wisdom, to keep the most important things uppermost in the mind of the saint.

The first of these standards shows Adam, Eve and the apple. Adam represents reason and the fight against fleshly sensuality, which is signified by the apple. Eve represents the temptation and sensuality that Adam resisted. Also on this standard is a golden lamb sitting in a tree: this symbolises humility and the victory of Jesus over the serpent. The lamb takes the highest place on this banner, because it was the blood of the lamb that washed away Adam's sin and routed Satan, the serpent.

On King Edmund's first banner, these symbols sit on a field of gules. The red symbolises the patience Edmund displayed when he was forced to fight the cruel Danes. To symbolise his many virtues as a king, the red background is sprinkled with bright golden stars and crescents.

Edmund carried this banner with him wherever he went, and because of the influence of our Lord Jesus Christ, the standard had the power to quench fires. Jesus granted this in recognition of Edmund's victory over the heat of fleshly lust.

This first banner will continue to preserve this land from enemies, and challenge their cruel pride. It will preserve our noble king, Henry VI, and will be carried by his side when he goes to war. With Edmund as his guide, his virtues can only increase, and his royal line will be enhanced. The grace of this martyr will make Henry so worthy that he will be registered among the nine worthies.

Edmund's other standard shows three golden crowns on a black background. The crowns symbolise his nobility, his virginity and his martyrdom. This standard was certainly the one Edmund took with him when he fought and killed King Swein at Gainsborough. By this miraculous victory, Edmund freed his kingdom from the necessity of paying tribute to the Danes, and increased his own power over his realm.

For our own King Henry, the three crowns symbolise his two kingdoms, of France and England, and the third crown he will surely inherit in heaven, where he will sit enthroned above the seven stars.

Now I must stretch my style to make it worthy of the task of remembering St Edmund; martyr, virgin and king: I will not be able to do it without St Edmund's help.

I will need all my skill to compile the details of his glorious life: his childhood, his royal ancestors, and his birth in Saxony. I have no flower or colours of rhetoric to illuminate his story, and I dare not call on Clio or any of the other muses for help, but I have read that grace, the king of the virtues, is better than eloquence. Grace has the power to instil prudence and direct all the other virtues. Grace is like a princess who has the freedom to correct such vices as sloth, which tend to impair wisdom. Without grace, every other virtue is barren.

I call, therefore, on grace to guide me, once Edmund has

let me through the gate into his life. Without grace, and Edmund's help, I will not be able to render his life into English.

First, I must record the royal date when I began this translation: it was the year when King Henry VI, lord of England and France, celebrated Christmas at Bury. It was at that time that Abbott William gave to me, his humble chaplain, the task of translating the substance of the noble story from Latin into English, to give to the king. This I agreed to do, out of obedience, though, as I have said, I am not eloquent.

BOOK I

Alkmond and Siware

1. Alkmond, Siware and Edmund

Once there was a king of Saxony called Alkmond. He was noble, manly, virtuous, rich and generous. He was noted for his prowess as a soldier, and for his hardiness and courage. He was very handsome, as wise as the god Mercury, and as victorious as Mars himself. He was also as watchful as Argus, and as circumspect as Scipio. He was famous throughout many lands, yet despite his good name he thought that true nobility lay in loving and fearing God.

Although he possessed worldly honour in abundance, and sat on a royal throne, he knew that God ruled over all earthly kings, and that a sceptre and a crown meant nothing if the king who possessed them did not love God with his whole heart and mind.

My source witnesses that this Alkmond had a wife. She was a worthy princess called Siware, a lady who was both beautiful and generous. She was also as meek as Esther, as firm as Judith and as loyal as Lucrece. The greatest of her wifely virtues was, however, her compassion. This she showed by joyfully giving alms, and visiting poor folk.

Together, King Alkmond and Queen Siware were like Abraham and Sarah, whose children were blessed by God.

Now King Alkmond had a dream in which he saw the two saints, Peter and Paul. This wonderful dream made him long to journey to Rome as a pilgrim. His journey to visit Peter and Paul was blessed with good fortune, and the king visited many holy relics in Rome.

While he was in the city, he lodged with a virtuous widow. This devout lady was looking at Alkmond one day when she saw a bright light shining in his breast. The beams of the light seemed to be divided in four parts, and the vision made the widow begin to prophesy.

'From your breast,' she said, 'a sun will come that will light up the four regions of heaven. This virtuous sun will shine like Phoebus in his chariot, riding high above the dusty clouds. It will gladden many countries with its light, which will grow and spread like a branch from you, King Alkmond. This sun will turn its heart to virtue, and in time to come, everyone will read about it.'

When he had heard the widow's prophecy, the king took his leave of her and returned home to Saxony. There he was received with joyous celebrations, because everyone was glad to see that he had returned safely.

In the same year, Siware fell pregnant by God's grace, and gave birth in the famous city of Nuremberg, eight hundred and forty-one years after Jesus was born. Her child's name was Edmund, which means 'blessed purity'.

With God's help, this Edmund grew in virtue as the years of his childhood passed. His expression was sober, his behaviour demure, and his face angelic. Everyone delighted in him, and he never offended anyone. He was a fine example of how good fruit comes from good trees, and crystal streams flow from a pure source.

His royal lineage became more and more evident as he grew to manhood, and his good qualities were a shining example to all. There was, however, no pride in him, and he spoke respectfully to people of both high and low degree. He did not disdain people just because they were poor: he was full of compassion for them. His behaviour showed humility, which is the king of all the virtues. He was also chaste, both in thought and deed, and always kept his word.

When virtue and love take root in a child when he is at a tender age, the roots go deep, and the plants cannot easily be pulled out. They continue to grow and thrive.

The widow's prophecy

2. King Offa of East Anglia

When Edmund was born in Saxony, East England was ruled by a worthy king called Offa. He was manly and virtuous, and renowned far and wide. He had ruled his kingdom for many years, but he had no heir to succeed him. For this reason, his heart was often heavy. Hoping that it might lighten his mood, Offa decided to go on a pilgrimage to the Holy Land.

Having first left his kingdom in good hands, Offa set off as quickly as he could. He decided to visit his cousin on the way, and as soon as he had crossed over to the Continent, he made straight for the kingdom of Saxony. There he was received as a monarch should be by his cousin King Alkmond. Many people from all the different parts of Saxony came to visit him, and his nephew Edmund was put at his service as a royal attendant.

Edmund served his uncle very attentively – in fact, he never left his side during his whole visit. The prince had a great affection for his royal uncle, and Offa did not fail to notice Edmund's merits. His wisdom and his reason told him that this nephew of his was likely to attain even greater virtue and nobility. As this charming youth continued to attend him day and night, Offa came to love him more than anyone he had ever known.

Offa was grateful to Edmund for his devotion, and the

fact that the young man was a close relative was always in his mind. He felt that it would be right for him to reward the love and service that Edmund had shown.

When everything was ready for Offa to continue on his pilgrimage, the spark of love in his heart prompted him to take Edmund in his arms and say, 'Good nephew, before I leave I wish all men to know that to repay you for your loyal service, I am giving you this ring. With it, I adopt you as my beloved son. I already love you with all my heart, as I would a son, better than any of my other kindred. This means that if I should die on my pilgrimage, you will inherit my kingdom.'

With that, Offa showed Edmund another precious ring, which had been given to him at his coronation by a holy bishop. 'Gentle nephew,' said Offa, 'this second ring will be a token or sign between us. If I should send you this ring with a message, you should know that the message is truly from me and nobody else. If the message should tell you to do something, do it faithfully.'

King Offa said all this with tears running down his face. As he made to leave, he embraced Edmund again and again as a true father would.

This was witnessed by Offa's cousin King Alkmond, who took careful note of everything the king from England said. Smiling, he said, 'Son Edmund, have you forsaken me? Will you ignore me now, and take a new father from among our close relatives? Since, in his goodness, he has adopted you as his son, he can provide for you from now on, and guide you with his advice.'

All the nobility of Saxony turned out to see Offa's leave-taking. There was pain at the parting of the two kings, but as we know, good friends cannot always be together.

After a grand send-off, Offa continued on his way, heading for the Great Sea. It is not part of my job to tell you about his journey, whether he sailed from Genoa or Venice, or what coasts his galleon sailed past. I have no idea whether their progress was fast or slow, and I certainly cannot describe the strange towns he visited, because these are not mentioned in my source.

I have never read or even seen the *Cosmography* of Francis Petrarch, where he describes all the strange places in that part of the world, and how sailors navigate on the Great Sea, so I can hardly describe any of that.

Suffice it to say, Offa reached the Holy Sepulchre, the object of his pilgrimage, and showed his devotion there. He stayed there several days, saying special prayers, and thus fulfilled his vow. With his heart full of gladness at having seen this place, he embarked again and headed home.

My source tells me that on his return journey, King Offa fell sick at a place called Port Saint George. As he lay in his sick-bed, he could tell that his condition was worsening, and he accepted that he was soon to die.

He made his last confession, to ready himself for death, and received the holy sacrament. He then ordered his whole retinue to come and listen to him, and when they were all assembled and kneeling before him, he began to tell them what was in his heart.

'Sirs,' he said, 'listen well. I will address the matter of who shall succeed to my kingdom after my death. To avoid all uncertainty, I am making my last will and testament now, and you must faithfully report what you have heard me say when you return to England. My successor shall be my cousin's son. When I am gone, take him this ring as a token as quickly as you can, and tell him to get himself crowned with all haste. Deliver this message as I have said it to you: if you change it, you will be disobeying me!

'Do not argue among yourselves about this, but work hard to quickly establish him in unfettered possession of my throne. He is the one I have chosen to be king after me, because of his many virtues. I see that his disposition is likely to make him even more virtuous as time passes, and God has already given him seemliness, wisdom and beauty in abundance. He loves and favours people of both high and low degree; and to see so many virtues met together in one person is wonderful. Therefore, in one word, he will be my heir.'

When Offa's retinue had heard all this, they were all bound by oath to carry out the king's last command. He handed over the ring, then weakened and died, making a blissful end and sending his soul to God's mercy.

After his death, Offa's followers did the best they could to bury him with honour and solemnity in such a strange and remote country. Once they had done this, they took to sea. They headed straight for Saxony, and made good speed, by God's grace. In just a few days, they were ready to give their message to King Alkmond.

They told him that his cousin King Offa had died well, and Alkmond began to weep as if he were turning to water. They gave Offa's ring to young Edmund, and begged him to make ready to sail to England straight away, to claim his inheritance. At this, Alkmond kept himself to his own chamber, and wore nothing but black. He refused to see anybody, until at last his sorrow began to slake itself.

The Saxon king called a council of his wisest lords to consult about what had happened. He asked them whether his son, who was so green and tender of age, should go to England to claim his heritage; and he reminded them that the presence of Edmund was his own chief joy in life.

King Alkmond's councillors answered with one voice that Edmund should indeed go to England and be crowned as if he were Offa's own first-born son. They discerned that divine grace had chosen the boy for this role, and said that it would be vain to resist God's plan: no counsel could prevail against it. They knew that God in his magnificence ordains the palm of princes, and the crowning of kings, in marvellous ways.

Alkmond's heart grew heavy at the thought of Edmund's departure, and wept, even though he remembered the woman who had seen the bright light emanating from his own chest, and prophesied that this light was Edmund, his son, who would shine with many virtues.

The Saxon king weighed these things in his mind, and saw that this change had come about through the will of God. Therefore, drawing on his reserves of wisdom and discretion, Alkmond consented to the petition of the English ambassadors.

Then he chose twenty of his wisest knights, and put them together with twenty of the knights who had accompanied King Offa to Jerusalem. From the forty, he picked one stalwart knight to act as young Edmund's protector. This celebrated man had long experience both of arms, and of the arts of peace, and always conducted himself with the utmost prudence. He could be both serious and mirthful as the occasion demanded, and in every way he was fitted to attend a king.

Alkmond also chose churchmen to advise Edmund in doctrinal matters, and chaplains to oversee the young king's early-morning prayers. He also chose virtuous squires and yeomen to serve his royal son.

The father then arranged for his son to have the very best of kingly apparel, and stuffed his ships with food and attendants. When they were ready to sail, Alkmond fell to his knees and meekly begged God and the Virgin Mary for their blessing on the voyage.

I need not describe the woeful sobbings and sighs that were heard at Edmund's parting, and I will not mention the the heart-piercing sadness that everybody felt. To describe the piteous weeping of Alkmond and Siware, which made them almost drown themselves in tears, is not part of my task, and I will not try the reader's patience with an account of how often Siware fainted.

This noble princess could not restrain herself, when she saw her son taking his leave, and she sobbed and wept and complained, even though she knew it grieved the young man. This is how all tender mothers show their love: they cannot help it.

The parting of Siware and Edmund was so bitter that when she hugged and kissed him, her face was covered with tears. When she saw him set off on the sea, she wept with uncontrollable pity.

All that day she stood and watched Edmund's ship, and where the ship had been, staring out to sea. Nobody could distract her or make her leave the place – nobody can love as much as a mother! When she had stood and mourned in that place long enough, she had to be carried home.

Offa on the sea

3. Edmund in England

The winds favoured them, the shipmen were expert navigators, God held his hand over them and they soon landed at a place called Maidenborough.

As soon as they landed, holy Edmund knelt down a short distance from his ship and prayed to God that his coming would be acceptable to him, and also beneficial to all the land. To show that he had heard his prayer, God made five springs well up in that place, which had been sandy, hard and dry before. These miraculous springs have long been noted for their curative powers – all sorts of strange maladies are healed by their power. By making these springs well up, the eternal God magnified the name of Edmund, his true knight.

Since Edmund first set foot in England, all the fields near where he first came ashore have been more fertile than any other land in that area: this is how God's grace works through his saints.

By the place where the springs welled up, Edmund had soon built a royal town, that still stands there today as a reminder of his coming. Today this place is called Hunstanton, which means, in Latin, sweetness and strength. 'Hun' means 'honey', for sweetness, and 'stanton' means 'stone,' a very hard thing.

The first citizens of this town, among whom were some of those who had brought Edmund from Saxony, earned this name because they were very humble and agreeable. Their behaviour was peaceable, but if they were challenged, they were manly defenders. In an attack, they fought like hardy champions, but though they were like lions in time of war, they were like lambs in time of peace.

After his arrival, Edmund stayed in this new town for nearly a year, and then he moved his household to the town of Attleborough. There he spent time memorising the psalms, while a plot was hatching to deprive him of his kingdom.

Certain enemies of the young man had entered the region, and were trying to discredit him, but, in the sight of God, truth overcomes power, and God himself promoted Edmund's claim, even though he was such a young man.

Hunbert, the Bishop of Elmham, knew all about the plot, and he summoned all the lords of the kingdom to a meeting, where he showed them King Offa's ring. A steward of King Offa was also present, and he explained and affirmed the meaning of the ring. Twenty knights who were at this meeting gave Hunbert their backing, and when everyone had been reassured about the rightness of Edmund's claim, they cried out with one voice that he was their true king.

At this meeting, a date was set for the young king's coronation, and Edmund readied himself at Attleborough. Soon a multitude of lords and worthy knights were leading Edmund in a grand procession into Suffolk, to be crowned at the royal town of Bures.

I have only black and white to colour my description of this royal event. I have never gathered flowers in the garden of Cicero, or slept upon Mount Cithaeron. I have never drunk at Helicon's well, or won favour from Calliope, so I hardly have the skill to describe Edmund's coronation.

On that day, which was none other than Christmas Day, by the power of God, he received a crown, a sceptre, a sword and a ring. Bishop Hunbert anointed him very solemnly, as it says in the chronicle.

The crown, which was set on his head, symbolised how he would rule his people through his high nobility. The sword was there to show how he would strike fear into the hearts of anyone who tried to oppress his subjects. The sceptre symbolised piece, and the ring, righteousness, both of which play their part in keeping a king on his throne.

All this happened eight hundred and fifty-six winters from the incarnation of God, at Bures, when Edmund was a handsome youth of fifteen.

Springs well up

41

4. Edmund is King

When his coronation, which included everything that was most fitting for such an event, had been accomplished, blessed Edmund assumed total control of East England, by God's will.

Guided at all times by the Holy Spirit, the young king established new laws for his kingdom, based on truth, equity and righteousness. In this and in other matters, he struck a balance between the sceptre and the sword – between mild peacefulness and the business of punishing reckless people with the sword.

Before he punished people who were guilty of rioting or other crimes, he carefully examined what they were accused of, and proceeded without haste. Wise men say that Discretion is the mother of all the virtues, and that her daughters, Reason and Providence, sustain her. Edmund worked hard alongside these three to do good for his kingdom.

He reigned in idle people and people who lived by theft, and cherished those who worked hard for the common good. He also cherished the princes who ruled under him, and imposed martial discipline on his knights, applying the doctrine of the famous Vigetius.

First and foremost, Edmund held the church to a high

standard of perfection. He made sure it was free of simony and hypocrisy, and only gave benefices and positions of authority to devoted, contemplative men of perfect life.

He was impatient of heretics, and made himself into a stick to beat them. He gave the Lollards no comfort, and hated false doctrines, adulation, divided hearts and sowers of discord.

He appointed prudent, well-educated judges who were quite free of corruption and the love of bribes. In this way, the light of truth shone out clearly, and nobody was allowed to dim it by brute force. Nobody lied under oath, and there were no dishonest jurors.

Trade was carried on honestly, and artisans were truthful about what they made. Nobody even understood what fraud meant, and workers were paid promptly at the end of each day, and never had to take out loans to tide themselves over.

In this way, Edmund ordered the church, the judges, the knights and the merchants of his kingdom with great perfection, so that together with him they made a fine image of how a kingdom should be run. Under the young king, princes oversaw the state with prudent, rational eyes, looking out for dissension and listening for injustice.

To defend the state, Edmund put knights in charge of his army, which protected virgins and widows and defended the church. In a just fight, he showed great prowess as a soldier, and became the very shield of knighthood and the glory of worthiness. Before the battle, he showed he had the manly prudence of Nestor in the matter of setting out his forces. In the heat of battle, he was skilled and mighty, and as hardy as Tideus. He often gained the sword of victory, then showed that he had Hercules' magnanimous heart. He divided the spoils of victory fairly, and gave bounteous gifts without delay.

For sport, and to avoid idleness, this prince would hunt

and hawk, and play at other honest pastimes. He would also train himself in knightly skills, such as riding and jousting.

Edmund ordered everything so perfectly that nobody had any reason to complain. The head of the state did not despise the foot, and they foot did not rebel against the head – the whole body was united in one love.

The king's own form was just as delightful. Whoever looked him in the face loved him straight away – he was so well-made, like a strong knight who was ready for any noble work. His behaviour matched his appearance – benign, prudent, patient and devoted to God. He was an example of virtue for everyone.

First thing in the morning, he would process with his knights to his oratory, to hear the service. In his spiritual life he was a devout contemplative, with every virtue locked up in his heart; and in the earthly part of his life he was a good knight.

In Edmund's court, there was no over-eating or keeping late, drunken hours. He did not shut his gate against the poor, and his treasury was always open to relieve their plight. His heart was moved by royal mercy, which inspired his to clothe the naked and feed the hungry. He also sent alms to poor people who were bedridden.

Who can hide a bright light when it is burning on a candelabrum? Who can dim the bright beams of the sun? Who could stop the fame of the holy Edmund, God's own knight and Christ's own man, spreading to many kingdoms?

The rumour began that in East Anglia there was truly noble, knightly king. News of him was read and sung in many foreign ports, until his noble fame reached Denmark. There the accounts of his knightly prowess, his chivalry, nobility and virtuous government provoked envy. Such qualities, when reported, always will make some people jealous and disdainful, especially if they themselves cannot attain to them.

I must now break off my narrative, and begin a kind of digression, to explain how the Danes first came into this region. After that, I can relate the manner of Edmund's martyrdom.

Coronation of Edmund

BOOK II

Edmund hunting

1. The Envy of Less Happier Lands

Once, in Denmark, there was a pagan king called Lothbrok. He loved to hunt and hawk, and when he had prayed to Mars he would devote himself to the service of Diana.

This Lothbrok had two cruel, spiteful sons called Ivar and Ubba. They were always at pains to stuff their ships with treasure, like pirates or sea-robbers. Like men who are mad to the heart, they always enjoyed killing and shedding blood. They did not care whether they prospered by fair or foul means.

Once, when they were sitting in the presence of their father Lothbrok, they began to boast, saying, 'Is there any king or prince alive today who is as famous and powerful as we are? Who is as confident, manly or noble as we are, the masters of the sea and the land? Nobody would dare to rank themselves above us. We are always victorious: we use our swords to steal from merchants and others, whether they travel by land or by sea, and we care not whether it be right or wrong. Who can claim to be as mighty as we are?'

When he had listened to them for a while, Lothbrok he began to smile at their folly, and told them to shut up. 'There is someone,' he said, 'a tender young man, who is so much better than you two that he is like the sun, and you are like a tiny star compared to him.

'He is a king, who reigns in East Anglia, and everybody speaks well of him. So you should give over your boasting! His prowess is so great that it transcends all your enterprises, as the moon transcends a cloudy sky. He is manly, but also wise, and he trusts in providence like a true knight. He governs well, and though he is strong, he is not violent. His fame trumps your foolish boasting. He is no time-waster, and though he is young, he passed his youth in Saxony very well. Now he sits on a dais like a true, famous king, while you two are just notorious thieves.

'So, tell me something you have done, either by land or water, that can match the noble deeds of this young king of East Anglia!'

When their father had finished talking to Ivar and Ubba in this scornful way, they felt jealous and also truly ashamed that Lothbrok should praise King Edmund like that. Soon they had hatched a conspiracy between them, and vowed to be avenged on Edmund if they could find an opportunity.

This shows how evil is always opposed to goodness, as the light of virtue is opposed to the vicious darkness. Perfection and ravenous violence are likewise always opposed, as are knightly prowess and dishonest pillage. It was inevitable, therefore, that Ivar and Ubba would hate Edmund.

Soon it happened that when King Lothbrok was out hawking, he deliberately outstripped his followers so that he could be alone. He found himself by a river, and got into a little boat. There he sat, all alone, and a mighty wind suddenly arose and drove his boat far out into the salty sea. There it drifted, with the Danish king aboard, for two or three days. Lothbrok was truly frightened, and could see no way to get to land. He was nearly shipwrecked on some sands, and endured several storms that tossed his little boat around.

At last he was cast up on the shore of Norfolk, near a

village called Reedham. The villagers thought he looked so strange that they took him to King Edmund as a curiosity that he might be interested in. How could a king suddenly appear here? they thought. Nobody could make out where he came from or who he was exactly, and as for himself, he kept his own counsel. Everyone could see that the strangers was pretty old, however, and behaved in a regal way.

Edmund's court always welcomed pilgrims and strangers, and when he saw the mysterious, shipwrecked king, he ordered his servants to comfort the man as well as they could. When it became clear that their guest was keen on hunting and hawking, Edmund detailed Bern, the master of his hunt, to serve him.

Although he had always been a pagan, Lothbrok found that he was soon full of admiration for his host's court, his prowess and knightly discipline, and his excellent beliefs. It seemed to the Danish king that the household where he now found himself was like a lighthouse designed to guide people to virtue. He therefore approached the English king and humbly begged him that he might stay with him in this earthly paradise, and serve him, for instance by carrying messages.

Edmund granted him his wish, and also gave him permission to hunt and hawk with Bern whenever and wherever he wished, and also to return to court only when he wanted to.

Now Lothbrok was an experienced hunter, famous for it in his own country, and his hawk took many birds every day, which the Dane brought back to Edmund's house. These included water-fowl and land-birds, and Lothbrok also showed his skill in hunting down other game. Soon the whole of Edmund's household was praising the Dane, except Bern the hunter, who grew jealous and began to plot the murder of Lothbrok.

Bern had no reason to hate the Dane, except that he was

better than he was at hunting; but one day, when they set out with their greyhounds into a forest to find game, Bern jumped on Lothbrok from behind, murdered him, and hid his body in the bushes. He then returned home, acting as if he was ignorant of what he had done in his fury.

When Lothbrok had been missing for a full day, Edmund began to inquire after him, but soon Lothbrok's greyhound rushed into the house, fawned on the king and began to whine piteously. Edmund gave him some bread, and then the dog ran straight back to his master's body, where it lay dead in the forest.

When nobody had seen Lothbrok for nearly three days, King Edmund grew suspicious, and made a serious inquiry into whether anyone had seen him.

On the morning after the third night, the greyhound reappeared, and again fawned on the king most piteously. Edmund ordered a knight to follow the greyhound when he left the palace, and the knight did so. Of course the dog returned to the place where Lothbrok's body was lying dead, and there the knight found the Dane's body, in a dark little valley in the forest, under a pile of leaves. His wound was still bloody, his face pale and dead, and his eyes ghastly. Beside him, his hound howled in mourning.

Murder will out, though it remain hidden for a while, and the murderer will be punished. It soon became clear, by certain signs, that Bern had done this deed out of insane hatred and longing for revenge. When Edmund was in command of all the facts, he addressed himself to Bern's punishment. He had him arrested, and sentenced him to be cast adrift in the sea in the same vessel in which Lothbrok had arrived – a craft without oar, sail or mast.

After he had been cast adrift, the wretched Bern's craft followed the winds, and was nearly broken apart by the waves. It was driven onto rocks and sands, and at last began to approach the coast of Denmark. By chance, Bern landed at exactly the place where Lothbrok had most loved to go hawking, when he was alive.

The Danes immediately recognised Bern's boat as the one Lothbrok had been swept out to sea in, although they knew nothing of where he had ended up, and had not heard about his death. Bern was immediately taken to the court of Ivar and Ubba, the two sons of Lothbrok who now ruled Denmark.

The two brothers immediately started to torture Bern, to find out what had happened to their father. The envious, snake-like Bern, who deserved to be hanged or whipped with chains, answered with a pale face that King Edmund had murdered Lothbrok.

'He did it out of envy and spite,' Bern told the brothers, 'and to insult you, your royal line, and your princely blood.'

2. The Danes Invade

When they had heard this, Ivar and Ubba believed Bern, and their rancour and cruelty made them quite mad. They resolved to be avenged on Edmund, and they gave orders that a great army should be gathered out of the whole of Denmark. They loaded twenty thousand fighting men onto the ships of their great navy, and set off for England.

Bern the hunter acted as the navigator and pilot for the whole fleet, but the winds were contrary and they were driven far to the north, to Berwick upon Tweed. They were forced to land there, and the Danish army was soon marching south, slaying Christian men, women and children on their way. It seems that they were determined to kill all Christians, and they sacked and looted all the churches and abbeys they came across.

In this way, the cruel, tyrannical brothers showed themselves to be opposed to the laws of God and nature. They were in England for several years, and they had no justification for what they did, except for blood-lust. After more years of cruelty had passed, Ivar decided to separate from his brother and go south, leaving Ubba in the North Country. He marched on East Anglia with a huge army, intending to attack Edmund.

When Ivar's host pitched their tents in Edmund's kingdom, the locals dared not oppose him, or disobey any of his commands. They moved from place to place, harassing and oppressing the young king's subjects. The Danish prince and his men killed everyone they met, including women and children: they would not hold back their swords because of pity, or the prayers of their victims.

After Ivar had pitched his pavilions on a plain near Thetford, he and his men entered the city and slew everyone they saw as they went up and down the streets. The people of the city had had no warning, and were quite unprepared. The Danes cut them down like unprotected sheep: the survivors ran away in all directions, and could not regroup to put up any defence.

Soon Ivar set about sacking and looting Thetford. He killed everyone, except for a few old folks whom he considered too feeble and close to death to be worth the killing. The Dane scared these limping citizens into telling him where King Edmund could be found. He also compelled them to tell him about Edmund's army, and forced some to guide him to the young king's house.

Because they feared death at Ivar's hands, these feeble old folks led the Danish army to where Edmund was staying with all his knights. Before they had made much progress, Edmund got wind of their plans and, like a royal knight, quickly set out with a stately host. The two armies met at dawn not far from Thetford, and battle commenced. The slaughter continued all day, until the sun began to set, by which time Edmund and his army had shed much pagan blood.

That day, Edmund was Christ's champion. He proved himself a manly knight, and also a lion, since his enemies fled like sheep out of his sight. Ivar was among those who fled, because where Edmund's sword cut the air, no pagan could remain alive.

The soil of the field was stained with blood, and the king's sharp sword turned red. Nobody could withstand

Edmund's blows, and many pagan dead were strewn about the battle-field. That day, many Christians also lost their lives, defending our faith.

Surveying the field as night fell, Edmund began to think about the consequences of shedding so much blood. I his mind, he examined the question from every angle. He knew that when pagans died their souls went straight to hell, where they would be trapped for eternity; and he also knew that even pagans were made in God's image. For a Christian, he thought, it is a terrible thing to see such slaughter: conflicts between nations, that lead to such loss of life, are a terrible thing. Then, though he was a manly, virtuous knight, the victorious king resolved never again to shed human blood: this vow he made for Christ's sake.

Edmund remembered how Jesus had shed his own blood on the Cross to pay the ransom for all mankind. He then rose again on the third day, for the sake of peace and mercy. Christ loved peace, and never fought against anybody. Edmund resolved to follow Him, and gave up violence for good.

3. Prelude to Martyrdom

When he was forced to flee the battlefield with all his men, cruel Ivar began to hate Edmund even more. He was determined to wreak his revenge on the young king, and a worm of envy, like a wicked serpent, began to eat his heart.

His forces were dispersed over the countryside, but he soon set about gathering them together. When Ivar's brother Ubba heard of his defeat at the battle near Thetford, he marched south with ten thousand men to swell the numbers of the Danes. The brothers held a council near Thetford, to plan their revenge. There they devised a proud, perverse message to send to the English king. This was quickly conveyed by a boasting knight with a melancholy face and a disdainful, choleric manner. He showed no respect to anyone but Edmund, to whom he knelt as he delivered his message.

'I bring you a message,' he began, 'from a mighty prince, who is most victorious by land and by sea. He is invincible, fearful and very martial. He is incredibly famous as a conqueror, so much so, in fact, that it impossible to describe him adequately in mere words. In short, this message has been sent to you by my lord Ivar.

'He orders you and advises you to set aside anything that will contradict his will. To save yourself, you must forget all ideas of rebellion, and follow his orders. You must give up your kingdom, pay him tribute-money, and rule as a king under him. You must also give him all your treasures, and give up the Christian religion. You must now sacrifice incense to his gods. Agree to this, and quickly – do not even think about saying no!

'In his mercy, Ivar will grant you an allowance, and, in effect, pay you with treasure to be a local sub-king. Do not think about rebelling against him – that way you will only lose your treasure, your kingdom and your life!

'That is all I have to say,' the messenger concluded. 'Consult with your nobles, and waste no time in devising your reply to this message.'

King Edmund was not angered by this message. As always, he was prudent, discreet, patient, manly and wise, and he called on a bishop who happened to be there to give his opinion.

The poor bishop was so terrified that he just stood there, perplexed. He could see that, if he gave the wrong answer, he might soon be killed or turned into a slave. He turned his pitiful face to the king, but could not speak at first because he was so astonished by the messenger's threats. He simply stood there, looking more and more fearful, until at last he broke out, 'You are not ready to fight another battle. But the enemy certainly *are* ready. If you disobey Ivar's commands, he will attack this castle. You do not have many troops here, or many supplies. I think you need to choose the lesser of two evils.

'You need not abandon Christianity in your heart. You can pretend to turn pagan, and bide your time until better days come round.'

The bishop said this because of the fear that had infested his imagination. He could see no way for Edmund to preserve his own life, except to pretend to surrender to Ivar's wishes. But blessed Edmund was not born to lie: it did not belong to his royal blood. His heart was always whole, not split in two, and he hated to think of two heads inside one hood. By manly force, he maintained one face and one way of behaving, and he decided not to take the bishop's advice.

'Bishop,' he said, 'it might seem like a good idea to pretend to surrender to Ivar, as you have suggested, but I think we need to weigh this matter in the balance with great care. If I follow your advice, I might win all the world, but would I not also be offending God?

'There is earthly wisdom, but also spiritual wisdom, and the two are different. Earthly wisdom might persuade men to murder their own neighbours to gain some advantage, but God's law forbids the shedding of blood.

'This proud legate, sent by a tyrant, says that I should give up my crown and my Christian faith, and become a pagan. But truth always triumphs over falsehood, and though tyrants may reign and flourish for a season, they soon face their own damnation, whether they expect it or not.

'Speaking now not as a king but as a man, I will live and die in the Christian faith. I will never forsake my lord, who died on the Cross for me, and for the sake of love and faith I am prepared to shed my blood for Him.'

The king then turned to Ivar's messenger, and spoke to him very gracefully and patiently. 'Draw near, ambassador,' he began. 'Return to your lord as quickly as you can, and tell him my answer faithfully and exactly. Tell him I would rather die than turn from my belief in Christ. Ivar says he will grant me three things: my life, my kingdom, and some of his treasure. But I have no need of wealth, and I would rather lose my kingdom and my life than displease God.

'In the faith of Christ I am free of oppression and extortion, whatever your proud lord may say. But I will not make war against Ivar again – I will defend the Law of Christ with humility and sufferance.'

The haughty knight Ivar had sent to the king reported his words, making it clear to his master that Edmund would rather be cut up into little pieces with sharp swords than give up his faith.

'He despises paganism,' the knight said, 'he thinks it would be outrageous for him to surrender, be he has no appetite for shedding more blood. For arms, he has only his heart, and he told me in plain language that he wants to die for Christ. He thinks that he can free his people from your power by laying down his life. It seems that he is weary of this world, and he has told his manly knights to stand down and give up the war, in the name of peace.'

Edmund turns to the bishop for advice

4. Martyrdom

When Ivar had heard what his messenger had to say, he set out with a huge force and besieged Edmund's castle like a mad tiger. The young king stood firm when he saw this, and maintained his determination to die for the sake of Christ. He ordered that no one should try to hold the tyrant back, or put up any defence. He commanded that the gates be kept open, and soon Edmund was captured and roughly dragged until he stood before Ivar, just as Jesus was brought before Pilate.

Sitting in state, the Danish prince wore an angry expression, and started to describe the Christian faith in the most scurrilous way. He then asked Edmund if indeed he followed that faith.

'Ivar, I know that you already know that I am committed to Christ, heart, body and soul. I will stay committed, whichever way the wind blows. I will never change my faith, for life or death, or for joy or pain. Whatever happens, I will not change. The promise of treasure will not divert me, or princely power or nobility. The threats of tyrants and felons cannot move me, and your menaces have no effect, even though they are backed up with great power. You can sharpen your sword and dismember me joint by joint, but believe it, it is beyond your power to change my heart. You can kill my body, but my soul is free from your power, and it will reign with Christ in glory. Do your best! I defy all idolatry and false gods!'

When he had heard all this, Ivar became almost insane. He ordered that Edmund should be tightly bound, then beaten with sticks right there in front of him. As his body began to bruise and suffer mortal wounds, the martyr only cried meekly and patiently to Jesus for help.

The accursed Danes then took Edmund, bound him to a tree and used him for target-practice. Soon the martyr bristled with so many arrows that he looked like a prickly sea-urchin. In this way, Edmund resembled another martyr, Saint Sebastian. His royal blood ran down his sides, but all he did was pray to Jesus. This is how martyrs gain their crowns of victory, and climb up to heaven, to reign there like kings.

The Danes, as fierce as lions, continued to shoot at Edmund with their sharp, barbed arrows. They fired more arrows into wounds they had just made, deepening them. In this way, Edmund became like one of the champions of Christ, who washed their garments in the blood of the Lamb [see Revelation 7:14].

Like a true martyr, the young king, bound to his tree, was pressed like a grape on the vine. Torn by mad tigers, every nerve and vein pierced, he still thought it was no pain to suffer for Christ.

When Ivar saw that he was stained all red, he ordered his knights to cut Edmund loose from his tree, and commanded them to cut off his head. The young king asked for a pause, so that he could pray, and he asked God for patience to bear his suffering, since that would show Ivar that he was not victorious.

When he had finished his prayer, Edmund stretched out his neck and his head was cut off. And so he died, king, martyr and virgin, and his soul flew straight to heaven.

The Danes left his body, that great treasure, where it had fallen, but took Edmund's head and threw it into some bushes, to hide it. But Jesus would not forsake the new martyr, and he commanded a wolf to guard his head. By acting as Edmund's faithful sentinel, the wolf was going quite against his own nature. Wolves are usually dangerous beasts, who will even become man-eaters out of greed and hunger. But Edmund's wolf grew tame, forgot his wildness and waited patiently, night and day, by the martyr's head, meek as a lamb.

This may seem strange, but nothing is impossible for God. Daniel was safe among the fierce lions, and the Bible tells us that John the Baptist lived in the desert among serpents and dragons, and never came to harm.

5. Afterlife

Soon after the death of Edmund, the cruel oppression of Ivar and Ubba became a little less intense, and a search party was organised to find the body of the holy king.

They soon found the martyr's body, but not the head. At this, they wept and sighed, then set about searching all the forests and valleys in the area, with horns and hounds, like a hunting-party. They cried out, 'Where are you, lord, our beloved king? Where are you, Edmund? Show us your heavenly face!' and they heard a voice answering, 'Here! Here! Here!'

The searchers followed the voice, and eventually came upon Edmund's head, guarded by the faithful wolf. They knelt and prayed their thanks to God for the miracle they had witnessed – the head of a dead man, that spoke! But such is the power of God, that made Balaam's ass speak and rebuke his master, and made a hart speak to St Eustace.

Those who had found Edmund's head were glad but also sorrowful. They took up their treasure with due reverence, and carried it to where the martyr's body lay. They put the two together, and by a miracle they united, and there was no join or scar visible on Edmund's neck. All that could be seen was a line, like a thread of purple, that God put there as a reminder of Edmund's martyrdom.

The wolf that had acted as Edmund's sentinel howled piteously when the head was taken from him, but he followed those who had found it tamely and sorrowfully. He was loath to part from Edmund, who was the source of all his joy. He stayed near the body after it had been re-united, howling in sorrow, but showing no fierceness to anybody. Only when Edmund's funeral was finished did he go back into the woods. He was never seen again.

The king was interred at Hoxne, in a small building. He had died at the age of thirty, on the twenty-second of December, 870 AD.

Book III

Edmund visits Sweyn

The Miracles of St Edmund

A hundred and thirty years after the death of Edmund, and a thousand years from the birth of Christ, trouble came to the land of Albion.

The king at this time was called Ethelred, and again the trouble was caused by the Danes. Out of ancient malice and cruelty, they made war on England, and their King Sweyn came to this land to try and win the war. The Danes had no right to anything here – their only justification was wilful tyranny. Sweyn claimed the throne itself, and set about slaughtering and burning, sacking monasteries and minsters, and robbing cities and towns.

The Danes oppressed married women, ravished widows and deflowered maidens. They disdained priests and despised monks and nuns. Sweyn extorted tribute with his sword, but Ethelred could offer no resistance in the face of his cruel violence. The English king fled to Normandy, leaving England desolate and without soldiers.

When Sweyn's infernal robbers demanded tribute of East Anglia, the people asserted that they should not have to pay, since their patron was St Edmund. Of course Sweyn's scavengers did not agree, and all the East Anglians could do to save themselves was to pray to their saint.

All the people, both rich and poor, prayed night and day,

and many made pilgrimages to Edmund, but they were forced to pay the tribute for ten long years. Reduced to terrible poverty, the people still kept vigil by Edmund's shrine, kneeling or lying prostrate, the women barefoot and weeping piteously.

At this time, the chaplain or chamberlain of Edmund's shrine was a pious old man called Aylwin. Edmund often came to Aylwin in his sleep, and discussed holy matters such as contemplation with him. They would speak of heavenly things, and Edmund would reveal spiritual secrets to Aylwin.

One night, Edmund appeared to Aylwin in a glowing white robe, as white as snow, powdered with bright stars. His face was so fair that it seemed heavenly, and his eyes were bright as suns.

'Quickly, take this message to King Sweyn,' said the saint. 'Tell him in my name that he must ask no tribute from my people. Under the wings of my protection, they are not subject to such things. Tell him to vex them no more, and to leave them in peace. Tell him to beware of pride, and to respect you, my ambassador. If he fails to respect you, and my message, tell him he will have to pay the price.'

When he woke up, Aylwin was afraid to obey Edmund, but he set off for Gainsborough to do the saint's will. God was his guide, and he declared his message openly to King Sweyn, point by point, and word by word. Sweyn disdained to listen to the old man, and told him to get out immediately, although it was nearly night-time, and never come back.

And so Aylwin found himself going out through the gate into the night, with nothing to eat and nowhere to stay. He found a grave-yard and lay down on a tomb-stone, despite his great age, and stayed awake most of the night, casting his eyes up to heaven and praying for a safe journey home.

Aylwin got safely to Lincoln, and found a better place to lay his head. There, towards dawn, Edmund came to him again in a dream and said, 'Don't worry, Aylwin! Pluck up your heart! All the sufferings of my people will be paid for, before you even reach home. God will send us better news soon: he will help me in what I plan to do.'

And so Aylwin resumed his journey home, and the next night at Gainsborough, Edmund appeared to the tyrant Sweyn in his castle. The saint had been conveyed there by an angel, and he glowed like Phoebus. He was dressed from top to toe like a knight, and he carried a sharp spear. His coat-armour was of a heavenly azure colour, with three golden crowns on it.

'Do you want tribute from my land?' asked Edmund, 'then here is the tribute due to tyranny!' And with that, the martyr gave Sweyn a fatal wound with his spear.

Sweyn cried aloud with fear, and woke the whole castle. Then he yielded up the ghost, and I know not where his soul went. This happened on the second day of frosty February, in the year 1014 AD. Later, the Danes preserved Sweyn's body in salt and took it back to Denmark.

Nobody should be surprised by this miracle, that Sweyn was killed in his own bedroom in the middle of the night. There is no obstacle that God's power cannot overcome, on earth or in heaven, by day or in the night. This victory in a bedroom was just as glorious as a victory on the battle-field.

At this time, a poor Essex man called Wolmar lay dying. Suddenly he spoke out and said, 'King Edmund has pierced the heart of Sweyn, to free us from the tribute! Rejoice!' and with that he yielded up the ghost. This was also a miracle, because Wolmar was deaf and dumb, and had never spoken a word in his whole life, up to that time.

After the death of Sweyn, the Danes never asked for tribute again, and any other tyrants who demanded tribute from Edmund's lands were quickly punished.

I can prove this with the example of Sheriff Leofstan,

who had no devotion to Edmund, and thought that any time spent hearing about his miracles was time wasted.

One day, he planned to sit in judgement as a magistrate near the martyr's tomb. The guilty woman he was about to examine sought sanctuary near the martyr's tomb, but Leofstan sent bailiffs to drag her away and bring her before him for her trial. Some priests who were performing divine service in the sanctuary tried to fight off the officers, but they were like ravenous hounds.

The woman cried out, 'Help, blessed Edmund! This sheriff will kill me for my crime! Your sanctuary is being violated!' But Leofstan would have none of it, and had soon sentenced the poor woman to death. But he never passed any more sentences: the tyrant was soon possessed by a fiend, who gave him pain in every corner of his body, and he quickly yielded up the ghost. I dare not say where his soul is now.

This is an example of how the martyr will punish those who rebel against him. By contrast, people who trust him are relieved and comforted: he ameliorates their suffering, and supports them in quarrels.

Once there were five malicious knights who entered Edmund's precincts in full armour, with their swords drawn to frighten anyone who might try to resist them. They stole horses out of Edmund's own stable, but as they passed out through the gate they all went quite mad.

When they had repented, confessed, been absolved and given gifts to Edmund's shrine, they devoted their whole love and devotion to the martyr.

There was also a man of Flanders who knelt down and pretended to kiss Edmund's shrine, but actually tried to bite off part of a small golden pillar. By a miracle, his teeth stuck firm and he was trapped. Only when the monks came and prayed Edmund for mercy was the man freed.

Once, a gang of eight thieves broke into Edmund's church at night. One had a ladder, another brought a crowbar, the third was good at picking locks, the fourth had a lever, the fifth a pickaxe, the sixth a spade, the seventh had a bag and the eighth was ready to use heat to melt gold and gems from the shrine. But Edmund knew about all their plans, so that when the shrine was opened up in the morning, the eight thieves were found inside, frozen like statues.

They were soon bound and fettered and thrown in prison, and the Bishop of the Diocese ordered that they should all be hanged. Soon Theodred, the bishop, was sorry that he had hastily ordered these cruel executions, and all the people fasted and did penance. For the rest of his life, the bishop suffered the pangs of conscience, and showed a sorrowful face to the world.

Once when St Edward was at Bury St Edmunds with the Danish king Osgothus, went quite mad when he heard the miracles of St Edmund read out. He had always hated Edmund, and he decided to dress up in gold and pearls and walk round the martyr's shrine all day with a sword strapped to his side, casting scornful looks at the shrine and criticising the saint's life, his passion and his virtues. As he stood blaspheming in this way, he suddenly fell to the ground, despite all his pride.

There he lay twisting and wallowing, like a man possessed by a demon, until the news of it came to the ears of King Edward. The holy king took pity of Osgothus when he heard the horrible, mad sounds he was making, and asked Abbot Leofstan to pray for his recovery. All the monks, the abbot and the king, formed a procession and knelt in prayer, and poor Osgothus was allowed to lie near Edmund's shrine.

He lay there for a long time, but eventually his madness abated and he was sane again. At last, restored to health, he knelt and gave thanks to God. He resolved to change his behaviour, and be meek and devout, and devote himself to St Edmund.

Pride and boldness often come to grief in this way. Witness the case of the priest who refused to give Edmund's body shelter when it was being transported to London: his house burned down!

Edmund was being moved so that his body would not be exposed to attacks from the Danes. Many miracles happened on his journey. When the monk Ailwin, who was escorting the body, reached Stratford, he found that the footbridge over the River Lea was too narrow. But he found that when the cart had two wheels on the bridge, the other two floated above the river, so that he could push Edmund across easily.

Ailwin, Edmund's body and all the people who followed the cart entered London via Cripplegate. Their entry was seen by blind people, and as they passed, lame people grew straight, and a woman who had been paralysed all her life was cured.

Edmund's body was in St Gregory's Church in London for three years, until Ailwin was told in a dream that he should take the martyr back to Bury. He asked Alphun, the Bishop of London, for permission to do so, and Alphun granted his request, but secretly planned to install Edmund in St Paul's.

One day the bishop sneaked into St Gregory's with three priests. They tried to lift up Edmund's coffin and carry it out, but it would not move. It had suddenly become as heavy as a great hill made of stone. The four men could not move it, so they called for more people, who used ropes and chains, but still Edmund would not move.

When everyone was completely worn out, and the bishop realised that he had been thwarted, Ailwin approached Edmund with great meekness and love, and begged the holy king not to forsake his own country. After he had said his prayer, the monk lifted up the coffin with no trouble at all. Full of dread and reverence, Bishop Alphun then led the procession that conveyed Edmund out of the city.

Along the way, any sick people who sought Edmund's help were quickly cured, and many miracles occurred. Everywhere, the people tried to make his journey as smooth as possible: they repaired broken bridges, swept the roads, strewed fresh flowers before the saint, and hung out coloured cloths on the walls.

At Stapleford, the party stayed all night in the best house in that village. There they were well-received and well-treated, and the lord of the place, who had for a long time been sick with a terrible illness, was cured. In gratitude, this man gave the manor of Stapleford and all its revenues to the church where the bones of Edmund now lie.

At last they came to Bedericsworth, now called Bury St Edmunds, where the people had long despaired because of Edmund's absence. Now, at his return, they felt glad and light-headed. Everybody brought the saint an offering, and prayed to him night and day, begging him to never leave them again.

APPENDIX I

John Lydgate's Prayer to St Edmund

To alle men, present, or in absence,
Which to seynt Edmund haue deuocioun,
With hool herte and dew reuerence
Seyn this Antephne and this Orisoun :
Two hundred daies ys grantid off pardoun,
Write and registred afforn his hooly shryne
Which for our feith suffrede passioun,
Blyssyd Edmund, kyng, martir, and virgyne.

Domine rex gentis Anglorum, miles regis angelorum,
O Edmunde, flos martirum, uelud rosa uel lilium, funde
preces ad dominum pro salute fidelium ! Ora pro nobis,
beate Edmunde, vt digni efficiamur promissionibus xpi !

Deus ineffabilis misericordie, qui beatissimum Regem

Edmundum tribuisti pro tuo nomine Inimicum moriendo vincere,

concede propicius familie tue : ut eo interueniente mereatur in se antiqui hostis incitamenta superando extinguere.

Per xpm dominum nostrum. Amen.

O Lord, King of the English race, soldier of the heavenly host,

O Edmund, flower of the martyrs, rose or lilly, pour out prayers to the Lord for the benefit of the faithful!

Pray for us, Saint Edmund, in order that Christ might act on these worthy promises.

Ineffable God, have mercy on us, who assigned Holy King Edward to conquer the enemy by death in your name,

grant that your Holy family might be well disposed to us: so that he might merit an intervention that may destroy our ancient foes by conquering them.

Through Jesus Christ our Lord, Amen.

(trans. Tim Dixon)

APPENDIX II

Sample Verse from Lydgate's Original Poem

Whan cruel Hyngwar maugre al his myht
Constreyned was the feeld to forsake
And with his meyne was I-put to flyht,
A dedly hatreed gan in his herte a- wake,
Hym to purueie a vengance for-to take ;
And heer-upon a werm most serpentyne
Of fals enuye gan in his herte myne.

Version With Modern Spelling

When cruel Hyngwar maugre all his might
Constrained was the field to forsake
And with his meyne was I-put to flight,
A deadly hatred gan in his heart awake,
Him to purvey a vengeance for-to take ;
And hereupon a worm most serpentine
Of false envy gan in his heart mine.

Select Bibliography

Carlyle, Thomas: *Past and Present (Collected Works Volume XIII)*, Chapman & Hall, 1843

Hegge, John and Webb, Simon: *The Legend of St Cuthbert*, Langley Press, 2013

Hervey, Francis (ed.): Corolla Sancti Eadmundi, John Murray, 1907

Houghton, Bryan: *Saint Edmund King and Martyr*, Terence Dalton, 1970

Lydgate, John: *Poems*, Oxford, 1966

Lydgate, John and Webb, Simon: *The Legend of St Alban*, Langley Press, 2016

Renoir, Alain: *The Poetry of John Lydgate*, Routledge & Kegan Paul, 1967

Webb, Simon: *In Search of the Northern Saints*, Langley Press, 2018

Weston, Jessie: *From Ritual to Romance*, Doubleday, 1957

Wolffe, Bertram, *Henry VI*, Yale, 1981

For free downloads and more from the Langley Press, please visit our website at http://tinyurl.com/lpdirect

36623993R00047

Printed in Poland
by Amazon Fulfillment
Poland Sp. z o.o., Wrocław